SOLOS
for the
VIBRAPHONE
PLAYER

Selected and Edited by
IAN FINKEL

ISBN 0-7935-3973-0

G. SCHIRMER, Inc.

DISTRIBUTED BY

7777 W. BLUEMOUND RD. P.O. BOX 13819 MILWAUKEE, WI 53213

ED. 2926

FOREWORD

The vibraphone is the most musical of all mallet instruments, and yet there is a dearth of serious music — such as the concerto or sonata— written for it.

Perhaps this is the fault of the players, many of whom are lacking in soloistic training. I am referring, of course, to the symphonic orchestral field and not jazz, which has several noted virtuosos such as Gary Burton and Dave Friedman.

This volume of transcriptions, I hope, is a much needed addition to the solo vibraphone repertoire. The material in it is to be played without vibrato.

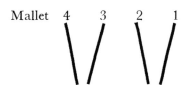

This book is dedicated to my teachers Walter E. Rosenberger and Norman Grossman, to whom I am greatly indebted.

I. F.

CONTENTS

		Page
JOHANN SEBASTIAN BACH	Aria	18
	Bourrée	19
	Minuet	18
	Minuet	19
	Seven Chorales	13
FRANCOIS CAMPENHOUT	Fugue	24
	Passacaille	25
FRANCESCO CORBETTA	Prelude in C minor	21
MUZIO CLEMENTI	Spiritoso (from: Sonatina No. 1)	32
A. ELMENREICH	Spinning Song	26
GEORGE FRIDERIC HANDEL	Fugue	4
	Spanish Royal March	6
JOSEPH HAYDN	Divertimento	30
FRIEDRICH KUHLAU	Allegro (from: Sonatina No. 1)	34
LUIGI LEGNANI	Caprice in C♯	10
	Caprice in D♭	8
	Caprice in G♭	11
LUIS MILÁN	Pavana	2
WOLFGANG AMADEUS MOZART	Allegro in F	15
	Minuet	16
	Minuet	16
JEAN-PHILLIPPE RAMEAU	Allemande	20
LUDOVICO RONCALLI	Preludio	3
GASPAR SANZ	Pavana	3
ALESSANDRO SCARLATTI	Gavotte	12
FERNANDO SOR	Allegretto	29
	Cantabile	28
	Divertissement	27
GEORG PHILIPP TELEMANN	Fantasia No. 7	6
ROBERT DE VISÉE	Prelude	20
SYLVIUS LEOPOLD WEISS	Preludio	23
	Sarabande	22

Solos for the Vibraphone Player

Selected and Edited by Ian Finkel

Pavana

Luis Milán
(c.1500 - 1563)

47205c

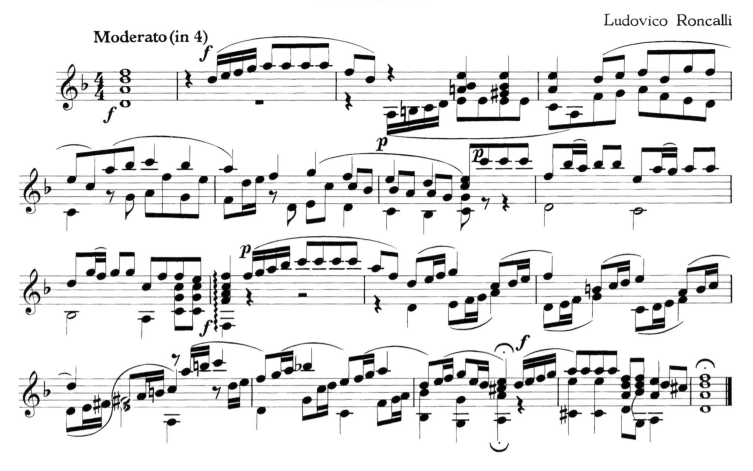

Preludio

Ludovico Roncalli

Moderato (in 4)

Pavana

Gaspar Sanz
(17th century)

Andante (in 2)

Fugue

George Frideric Handel
(1685 - 1759)

Spanish Royal March

George Frideric Handel

Fantasia No. 7

Georg Philipp Telemann
(1681 - 1767)

47205

Caprice in D♭

Luigi Legnani

Caprice in C♯

Luigi Legnani

Caprice in G♭

Luigi Legnani

Allegro maestoso

Gavotte

Alessandro Scarlatti
(1660 - 1725)

Seven Chorales

1 Meine Seele erhebet den Herrn
(My Soul doth magnify the Lord)

Johann Sebastian Bach
(1685 - 1750)

2 Herr Gott, dich loben alle wir
(To God let all the human race)

3 Du Friedenfürst, Herr Jesu Christ
(Lord Jesus Christ, the Prince of Peace)

14

4 Liebster Immanuel, Herzog der Frommen
(Dearest Emanuel, Lord of the faithful)

5 Christus, der ist mein Leben
(My Life is hid in Jesus)

6 Herr Christ, der ein'ge Gott'ssohn
(Lord Christ, by God Engendered)

7 O Haupt voll Blut und Wunden
(O Sacred Head Now Wounded)

47205

Allegro in F

Wolfgang Amadeus Mozart
(1756 - 1791)

Minuet

Wolfgang Amadeus Mozart

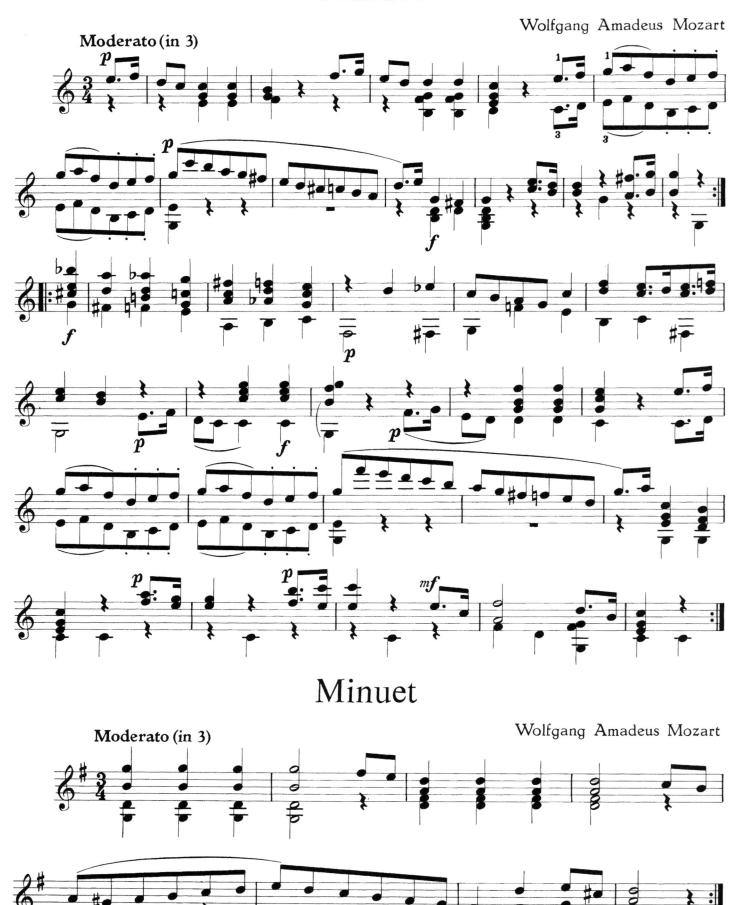

Minuet

Wolfgang Amadeus Mozart

Trio

Fine

D.C. al Fine

Aria

Johann Sebastian Bach

Andantino (in 4)

Minuet

Johann Sebastian Bach

Moderato (in 3)

Minuet

Andantino (in 3)

Johann Sebastian Bach

Bourrée

Allegro (in 2)

Johann Sebastian Bach

Prelude

Robert de Visée
(c. 1650 - c. 1725)

Allegretto (in 4)

Allemande

Jean-Phillippe Rameau
(1683 - 1764)

Moderato (in 4)

Prelude in C minor

Francesco Corbetta
(1620-1681)

Sarabande

Sylvius Leopold Weiss
(1686 - 1750)

Preludio

Sylvius Leopold Weiss

Fugue

François Campenhout
(1779 - 1848)

Moderato (in 2)

Passacaille

François Campenhout

Spinning Song

A. Elmenreich

Divertissement

Fernando Sor
(1778 - 1839)

47205

Cantabile

Fernando Sor

Allegretto

Fernando Sor

Divertimento

Joseph Haydn
(1732 - 1809)

Spiritoso

from: Sonatina No.1

Muzio Clementi
(1752 - 1832)

Allegro (in 4)

Allegro
from: Sonatina No.1

Friedrich Kuhlau
(1786 - 1832)

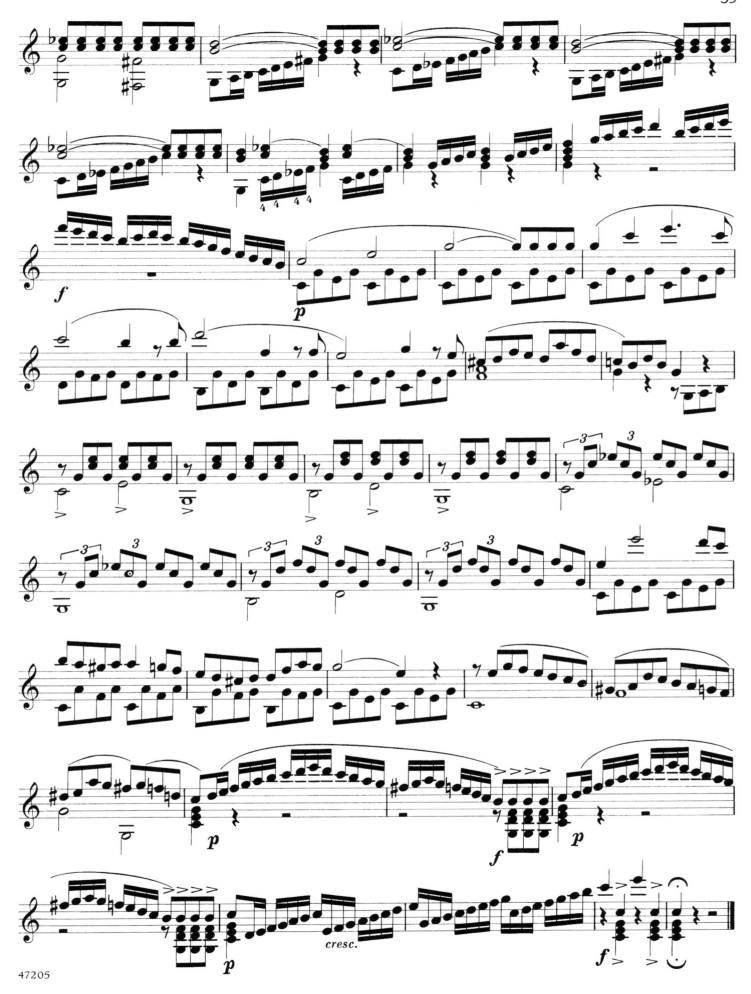